ONE OF THE SI

WESLEY'S ESSEX (

THE
TERRIBLE TREASURE HOLT
STORY

WITH ALL IT'S MYSTERIES, GHOSTS, HAUNTINGS AND INTRIGUES

Plus

30 STORIES OF GHOSTS AND HAUNTINGS IN AND AROUND THE CLACTON AND COLCHESTER AREAS

WESLEY H. DOWNES

£3.95

Copyright ©   W.H.Downes   1993

ISBN 0 9519289 3 7

All Rights Reserved

No part of this publication may be reproduced, stored in a
retrieval system,or transmitted in any form without prior
written permission from the publisher.

Published by Wesley's Publications, 6l Lymington Avenue,
Clacton-on-Sea,Essex CO15 4QE.

First Published l993.

Front Cover and Drawings by Rose Bishop.
Printed by Guild Press (Clacton), Clacton-on-Sea, Essex.
Typesetting: Guild Press (Clacton), Clacton-on-Sea,Essex.

AUTHOR'S ACKNOWLEDGEMENTS.

I am greatly indebted to all who have contributed stories and
information so freely to me, and duly acknowledge the authors
of previously published works.

I also wish to thank George who has assisted generally in
reading and correcting the manuscript.

Extra special thanks to Mr & Mrs Charles Sambridge for their
co-operation and for allowing 'The Terrible Treasure Holt
Story' to be written about their home.

INTRODUCTION

This may well prove to be one of the strangest books you have ever read. Generally based on fact, some proven, some probably still yet to be proved, some history, some with perhaps just a little poetic licence, some unbelievable, some plausible,some you the reader may consider downright impossible - that is what makes TREASURE HOLT what it is - a house of mystery and intrigue.

Even the writer's introduction and interest in Treasure Holt started one evening as a result of a mysterious telephone call.

A serious sounding lady's voice said she had been given to understand that I was interested in the occult, and that she had been requested to give me a parcel - left to her by an aunt - "as I would know what to do with the contents". This was in the late 1960's.

Intrigue made me agree to travel to Dovercourt the next day to collect this mysterious parcel.

Returning home and apprehensively opening the brown paper package, I was surprised to find a number of faded sheets of paper covered with pencilled writings and drawings. The paper was obviously the back of placards, normally displayed outside newsagents shops.

Carefully unfolding them, it soon became apparent that they would take a lot of deciphering, for not only was the writing continuous, but some of the pages were dated as if written in the 1930's, making them over thirty years old!

But what was also apparent, was an intriguing story concerning TREASURE HOLT written by a lady in a psychic trance, complete with the most beautiful drawings of buried treasure hidden in the grounds.

After many years of deciphering and painstaking research, I feel that at last, most of the TREASURE HOLT STORY can be revealed, and maybe with time, even more of its mysteries can be exposed and will help to confirm what at present appears to be just figments of imagination!!

Enjoy your reading.

W.H.D.   1993

CONTENTS

THE TERRIBLE TREASURE HOLT STORY

MORE HAUNTINGS

A photograph taken of Treasure Holt in the 1930's

The Author with Mr. & Mrs. Sambridge, the Owners, with 'Treasure Holt' as a background, 1992

6

THE TERRIBLE TREASURE HOLT STORY

TREASURE HOLT IN THE 1990'S

This is a story of a house, not just an ordinary building, but a house with a past, a terrible past. If the old twisted oak beams could talk, they would certainly tell just some of the dreadful deeds that have been committed within the walls and the surrounding grounds, ranging from murder, witchcraft, intrigue, hidden treasure, to ghosts and hauntings.

Formerly known as Perles Farm, TREASURE HOLT, as it is known today, stands isolated, surrounded by trees and meadows. The only access is a winding country lane which leads in one direction to a town just two miles away past the town cemetery, the other leads on to desolate marshes only a mile or so from the Essex coast; in other words, a perfect setting for what could be described as a writers paradise.

The present day house is unique in itself. Built in many styles and periods that are very difficult to date, the old creaking name sign, dangling crazily from a gibbet style post at the end of the driveway says 1138, but who knows what existed before this date?

Even to this day, in this modern age, there is no main water supply, gas, or mains electricity, and no main drainage either.

As a matter of fact, the previous owner was an eccentric bachelor of some seventy plus years, whose only companions were two foxes he had brought up from pups, and even they would only eat tinned meat!

If, on an autumn afternoon as the sun lowers behind the baring trees, one stands in the now overgrown grounds, a shiver will run up and down the spine. Even in mid summer there is that eerie coldness surrounding the whole area, and if you let your imagination wander --- well, you may well see some, certainly not all, the murky past floating before you.

Over the years many stories and legends have built up about this old house, some so spine chilling that mothers will not even allow their children to walk down the lane, let alone enter the driveway. Older parents still remember the horrific stories their parents told them when they were children.

So much interest has been shown in this old house over the years, that in the 1920's the Society for Psychical Research carried out an investigation into some of the hauntings. Again in 1972 the house was featured on B.B.C. Television's Look East programme featuring haunted houses. In 1992 B.B.C. Radio Essex featured Treasure Holt in one of their series of programmes on Essex hauntings.

Numerous newspaper articles have been written about it, and its history often related in magazines. Yes, 'Treasure Holt' is indeed a real treasure chest.

THE DAYS OF THE INN

Going back many years, long before Treasure Holt was a private house, even before it was a tumbled down farmhouse, it was an old Inn, set in what was then a heavily wooded forest. There was not even a lane leading to it, just a muddy rutted cart track and a couple of rough pathways through the forest, used by travellers on horseback and just a few on foot.

It was about this time that our story really begins, the date - - - well, let's just say - - about then.

Here was an ideal location for smugglers to carry on their illicit trade with little or no interference from the Revenue men and to this end it was certainly well used. Not many weeks went past without some form of contraband being brought from the seashore, across the marshes, either on donkeys or packhorses , along barely trodden trails, through the woods to the Inn, where they could safely store the goods or meet with contacts who would dispose of them with no questions asked.

During this period, the Inn was run by a husband and wife who were reputed to be a really evil couple in every respect. The Inn became notorious and was known to every thief, rogue and villain for miles around. It was equally well known as being a centre of witchcraft and Black Magic, with the innkeeper's wife the main witch.

When meetings were held at the Inn, interested people often travelled for two or three days either on foot or by horse just to attend what was usually a three day affair. Such was the attraction of witchcraft to the simple people at the time.

The innkeeper and his wife brewed most of their own very potent 'beers' and wines, so quite apart from any smuggled wines and liquors that came their way, there was never any shortage, their stocks were always kept well up by grateful smugglers, not only for storing the contraband, but for keeping their mouths shut and their eyes open for any strangers whose presence might mean trouble.

A tunnel had been constructed, starting under the floor of the stables at the back of the Inn, one outlet rising a short distance away in the grounds behind a thicket, and another branch heading towards the cemetery some distance away, but this was either never completed or collapsed after some distance had been excavated. Never-the-less, it was still a very useful hiding place for the hunted and for goods.

Of course, it was impossible to keep a place like this a secret for long. Rumours, often exaggerated, spread far and wide by word of mouth, meant that even some of the wealthy merchants, thinking they might increase their fortunes, found their way there and obtained some of the goods. There was always a ready market for anything smuggled because the taxes on legitimately imported goods were so high.

It was these wealthy merchants that the innkeeper and his wife really welcomed. Because of the nature of their visit, and the fact that they would be carrying large sums of money, these merchants did not let it be known that they would be travelling through the forest. The danger of being waylaid by highwaymen and footpads was very great, and life was cheap.

When a merchant eventually found his way to the Inn, he would be greeted with a strong drink and a hearty meal 'on the house', and his horse would be taken to the stables behind the Inn for a well earned rest.

Travelling was very slow and tortuous both for humans and animals. In the winter the tracks were muddy and slippery, in the summer they were very hot and dusty so, either way, the drink and food was more than welcome after a journey and it was of this fact that the innkeeper and his wife took full advantage.

A generous drink of home brewed ale, followed by an equally generous glass of the best smuggled geneva soon made the weary traveller feel very tired and it was at this stage that the crafty old landlord would suggest that, as he was not expecting any of the regular customers with whom the merchant was hoping to do business, to arrive until well after nightfall, perhaps he would like to retire to the best bedroom in the Inn, and he would send his wife up with a final glass of drink, and would give him a call when his prospective business contacts arrived.

This offer was nearly always taken up. The 'final drink' which the wife took up to the unwary traveller, was often just that. It would be a well and truly laced mixture, guaranteed to send anybody into a deep sleep. After a while, when the innkeeper felt that his 'guest' was sound asleep, he and his wife would go into the bedroom and search through his clothes and bags until they found his money. Now, they were very cunning, they never stole all the money, just a large amount, and of course, if the unfortunate man should complain next morning they would say that, whilst he was drunk, he bought the services of the wife, and if he was in such a state that he could not remember what took place, that was his misfortune, so long as he had sufficient money left to pay his bill.

However, if the unfortunate merchant had not been in a deep enough sleep when they were going through his belongings and woke demanding to know what they thought they were doing, the landlord would then produce a hefty club and hit the man over the head knocking him unconscious, or possibly killing him with the blow. Either way, it made very little difference, the result would be the same. In the floor of the bedroom, beneath a piece of rush matting was a trapdoor which, when raised, gave access to the room below. The innkeeper would go downstairs into this room, pull back more rush matting, exposing another large trapdoor almost directly below the one in the bedroom above; he would then open this ground floor trapdoor, to reveal a deep, foul smelling well.

At this point the wife would push the victim's body through the top trap, straight down into the well. This operation had been carried out so many times over the years that they had got it down to a fine art and the disposal of the clothes and bags was no problem either, these would always fetch good money when traded off to the smugglers.

Even to this day the trapdoor remains and directly below it there is a large concrete slab in the floor covering what still could be a well. Strange to relate, whilst the B.B.C. television cameras were filming there in 1972, a Spiritualist medium, not knowing the past history of the house, was walking about the room and stood on the slab. Suddenly he shuddered and said that he was picking up some awful vibrations from this spot and felt that something terrible was associated with it!!

It is said that some years ago this well was exposed, drained and cleaned out. It was over forty feet deep, and the remains of dozens of human bones, several old leather button up shoes, (all male) leather belts, some leather buckets, old rusty swords and a couple of flintlock pistols were recovered.

This well was then sealed up with a heavy concrete slab.

In 1928 when a part of the floor in one room was being replaced, workmen unearthed parts of a human skeleton, some buckles, pieces of clay pipes as used for smoking, some coins and a token, also other badly decayed items. The whole appeared to have been covered with a lime substance.

The token, when it was cleaned, revealed the name of 'John Wilkins Iron Master 1793', the buckles were identified as shoe buckles. **

There are many questions that will probably never be answered. Who was this unfortunate man who must have met his death at the Inn. Could it have been another wealthy merchant, if so, why not use the well as before? Could it have been a smuggler, possibly killed in a fight? Could it have been the landlord who had been caught out at one of his tricks? If so why bury the body under the floor, it would have been far easier to have taken it outside into the grounds or even into the woods. This is just one more mystery about the house.

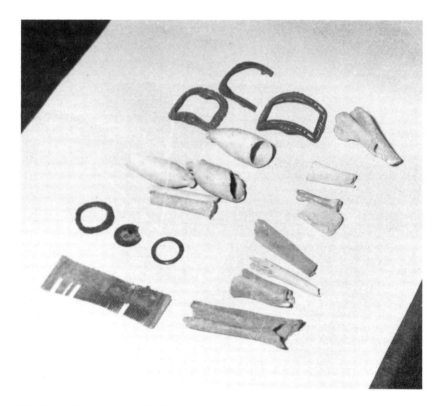

** See reference at end of story.

SIMON THE MONK MEETS KING CHARLES 1

Reverting to the period of Charles 1 who was on the run and in hiding from Oliver Cromwell and his Roundheads, we find that the King, together with a few of his trusted followers, had found their way to this lonely corner of the country and thought that the Inn was well suited to their purpose.

They could rest for a while and contact some of their sympathisers in this area; after all, Cromwell would not think of looking here for him. It seemed an ideal place.

Little did the King and his men know of the reputation of the Inn, nor of the infamous innkeeper and his wife.

After the King had been at the Inn for a few days, word of his whereabouts got around and he had a visit from a Monk by the name of Simon, who came from a monastery some six miles away. He had been sent by the Prior to contact the King and pass him some vital information.

The King received Simon and invited him to have a meal with him and his advisors, during which they listened to Simon's information with great solemnity. Apparently word that the King was staying at the Inn had now reached one of Cromwell's commanders who was gathering forces to surprise him.

Shortly after the meal, the King ordered his party to prepare to move without more ado to a safer hiding place that Simon had told him was being prepared for them.

SIMON'S CONVERSION

After the King had left, Simon thought that this would present him with a fine opportunity to have a talk with the innkeeper and his wife to try to get them to mend their ways.

Seeking them out and in an attempt to appear friendly he accepted their offer of some wine but, not being used to such potent liquor, he soon succumbed and had to be given a bed in order to sleep it off.

After a nights' sleep Simon still felt awful. The landlord's wife, hearing him move about the room, brought him a plate of food, which he promptly refused.

Seeing the condition poor Simon was in, she persuaded him that he was not yet fit enough to make his return journey and suggested he stay for a few days in order to recuperate. Simon, thinking that he might be able to carry on where he had left off trying to convert the couple, and in so doing his time would not have been wasted, readily agreed.

Having spent most of his morning lying on his bed, Simon had time to reflect upon his situation and of the traumatic happenings of the previous day. He started to think of ways he could turn this adversity to his advantage. After a while, he thought that if he went downstairs and tried to carry on with his plan to reform the couple, he might have more success this time, so, in the middle of the afternoon he gingerly made his way down the old creaking stairs.

Hearing him coming, the couple greeted him and asked if he would like something to eat or drink. He refused the food, but said that he would welcome some water as his throat was dry and he still did not feel too well. At this, the wife remarked that she had the ideal remedy for just such trouble, in fact it was an old herbal remedy, but she did not tell him that it would also contain a generous measure of strong geneva.

Returning from the scullery with a jug of the mixture and a goblet, she told him to hold his breath and drink the first one down in one go, which he did; he then said that his throat felt better already.

After a few minutes and another drink, he felt a warmth spreading throughout his body which gave him confidence to think about the question of their behaviour once again.

As soon as he could, he gradually worked the conversation around to their evil ways and suggested that they should think about their future before it was too late. They argued that they were not as bad as their reputation made them out to be, and perhaps he would consider attending one of their meetings to judge for himself.

Having fallen into their trap, Simon had no option other than to accept their challenge. Still feeling very shaky from the day before, and having emptied the rest of the mixture in the jug, he was in no fit condition to put up any further argument and was quite happy to be led back to his bedroom.

The next meeting of the Devil Worshippers had been arranged for the following week, and in the meantime Simon the Monk stayed on at the Inn where the innkeeper and his wife steadily plied him with drinks and lost no opportunity to indoctrinate him in their ways.

By the time the fateful day of the meeting of the Satanists dawned, Simon was well and truly ensnared in their web. The wine, geneva, their persuasive tongues had been very effective. Instead of Simon converting them, the boot was on the other foot, the couple had succeeded in converting him, but at this stage he was in no condition to realise it.

During the meeting, which was held round a fire in a clearing in the forest close to the Inn, he was constantly plied with more and more wine and what with the chanting, the excitement and the dancing, with the heat beating on his cheeks, he managed to climb on to a large fallen tree trunk. Standing there with his arms waving high in the air, he cried out that "he was forsaking his Church, his God, and his Faith and all that he had previously stood for and wished to become one of them - a disciple of the Devil, to practice Evil, worship Evil and to spread Evil." After this meeting it did not take him long to become a drunken sot.

Simon was not content with just throwing in his lot with them. One night, during one of the many drunken orgies held at the Inn, he boasted of all the wealth in gold plate and gold ornaments he knew to be in a nearby church, also the amount of gold in all forms in the monastery from where he came. With his knowledge as to where it was kept, how easy it would be to steal it: after all, he still had the keys to the side door of the monastery, nothing could be easier.

SIMON - - GANG LEADER

Simon was egged on not only by the innkeeper and his wife who by this time had become the closest of friends, but also by a French smuggler by the name of De Courcey, a frequent visitor to the Inn. Between them they made plans to steal as much of this gold as they could; De Courcey saying that he could easily take the gold back to France, where he would be able to obtain the best price with the least risk of being caught. Who after all would ever think of gold, having been stolen in England would be sent to France to be sold.

Some nights later, when the moon was very bright, Simon, who had been automatically elected leader, De Courcey, the innkeeper and three other smugglers, set off to walk the six miles to the monastery. Simon, who had walked this path through the forest so many times before, led the way.

Reaching the monastery wall, Simon led them to a small wicket gate used only by the monks. Slipping silently through, they made their way to the side door of the chapel to which Simon had the keys. Opening the door quietly, he led them straight to a small room where gold plate, candlesticks, chalices, salvers etc. were stored. Having found some wicker baskets, they loaded them with as much as they could carry, then struggled out the way they came in, Simon locking the door behind them, thus hoping it might be several days at least, before the loss was noticed.

Having spent far more time than they intended, not only on the journey but also loading the baskets, and then finding that the weight was much heavier than they had bargained for, they then spent even more time trying to sort out which items they thought were the most valuable. The whole escapade had taken most of the night and with daylight just beginning to break, they decided it would be too risky to be seen carrying heavy baskets away from the monastery, especially as the monks were known to be early risers. They therefore decided to take what they had already packed as far as the edge of the forest and hide it in the bushes, then return the next night to collect it.

Having successfully achieved the first part of their plan, they returned to the Inn where they had a meal and rested for the remainder of the day.

Later that night they returned to where they had hidden the treasure, finding it easily. They then made their way slowly back to the Inn where they took it straight into the stables and hid it down the tunnel, the entrance to which was cunningly concealed.

After making sure that everything was cleared and the tunnel entrance was once again hidden from prying eyes, they went into the Inn itself to have what they considered a well earned drink and to talk over their arrangements to carry out the next part of their plan, which was to rob the church near the monastery.

Having decided that the robbery at the monastery had not yet been discovered, they thought it might be best if they went and robbed the church the next night before any alarm at all was raised.

They rested for the remainder of that day, then at nightfall, collected the hidden wicker baskets taken from the monastery and retraced their steps through the forest once more.

Reaching the church without mishap, they easily forced a door and proceeded to load the baskets with as many gold ornaments as they could carry. Heavily loaded with their ill-gotten gains, they wearily made their way back to the Inn just as daylight was breaking. Arriving without being detected, they once again made their way straight to the stables and the tunnel to hide their spoils. Having satisfied themselves that everything was safely hidden, they retired to the Inn where again a welcome drink and food awaited them.

With success going to their heads, having so far plundered a monastery and a church within a matter of a few days with no alarm being raised, they decided they could well take the risk to rob a church in a town some ten miles away Simon knew to be very rich with gold contents. To do this would mean travelling by horse and although none of them were expert horsemen, they all agreed that by taking the journey steadily they were confident they would be equal to the task.

Having decided to travel most of the way in daylight, they left the Inn late in the afternoon in order to arrive at the church by nightfall. If they should be seen approaching the town they would be taken for six weary travellers seeking shelter for the night, which would not be an uncommon sight.

Once again all went well. Arriving at the church just as darkness fell, they walked their horses a short distance to where they could be tethered securely to some trees. Then each removing the two large bags that were slung from either side of his horse and once again forcing a church door, they quickly disappeared inside.

Working by the light of shaded rush lanthorns they soon filled their packs with ornaments of all kinds. When they thought they had as much as they could safely carry in the darkness, they loaded the horses and walked them slowly away from the church, making as little noise as possible.

When they were a safe distance, they mounted and cautiously made their way back to the Inn.

The whole operation went perfectly for them. Nothing was hurried and there was no reason to even suspect that the robbery would be discovered for at least a few days.

Arriving back in broad daylight, they made their way as before to the stables to hide their latest hoard in the tunnel. Then into the Inn to celebrate their successes and to discuss the question of disposing of the loot.

ENTER AND EXIT MATTHEW

Whilst they had been hiding the stolen ornaments down the tunnel, Simon and the others did not realise that they had been watched byMatthew, a little man who worked at the Inn doing odd jobs and helping in the kitchen. He always wore a tall 'sugar loaf' hat and an old brown suit of clothes about two sizes too large for him. Now, Matthew was not a bad man and took no part in the goings on at the Inn, but he was afraid of the innkeeper and his wife, and only stayed there because they gave him food in return for his labours, and let him sleep on the straw in the loft of the stables. It was from there that he saw them hiding the gold.

Matthew had overheard some of their conversation when they were planning to steal from the monastery and the churches and now he had seen where it was hidden. A plan was forming in his mind and although he did not often think, now his brain was working overtime. Had he got the nerve to go into the tunnel and take some of the golden ornaments etc., hide them in a place where only he would know, then later try to return them to the church. Yes, he told himself, he could, and would.

Waiting until all was quiet inside the Inn, he crept down from the loft, quietly lifted the trapdoor and entered the tunnel. He did not have to go far before coming to the gold. He then made three or four journeys from the tunnel to the loft, taking as much as he dare without it being missed, and hiding it under the straw where he slept. On his last trip he picked up a small wooden box and on looking inside it, found that it was nearly full of golden guineas. This, he thought would be his as a reward for saving so much of the churches' gold. Carefully replacing the trapdoor and spreading some loose straw over it, he went back to his warm place amongst the straw .

The next day, Matthew was the only one left at the Inn, all the others having gone about their business and the landlord and his wife gone to get more supplies of food. Seizing this opportunity, he went to the loft, picked up the box of guineas and brought it into the Inn. Going to a trapdoor in the floor beside the fireplace, he raised it and went down the steps and hid the box on a shelf behind some old brandy kegs, then, returning to his kitchen job, carried on as if nothing had happened.

Alas, poor Matthew was not destined to benefit from his efforts, however good the intent. Later that day a yelling mob came to the Inn looking for his master. They had found out that the innkeeper was involved with the robberies, and they wanted the gold back and revenge. Matthew tried to tell them that he was the only one there, but they would not listen, and pushing him to one side, they swarmed into the Inn, ransacking as they went from room to room.

When they eventually realised the innkeeper was definitely not on the premises, they turned their wrath on the unfortunate Matthew. Chasing him as fast as his little legs would carry him, they threw stones at him, until one very large one hit him on the head causing him to fall. They then continued to kick and beat him until he died.

It is strange, but like a lot of other stories, this one is no exception in that anyone who handles stolen church property will die a violent death. It is almost as if an automatic curse is put on it!!

It is also ironic, that the innkeeper's wife - the old witch, also lost her life violently. She became involved in a fight with a company of Cromwell's Roundheads who, some weeks after he had fled, searched the Inn in course of the hunt for King Charles I.

SIMON HITS ROCK BOTTOM AND MEETS HIS END.

(WARNING!! This Chapter is HORRIFIC.)

During the time that all the robbing and stealing had been going on, Simon was mostly in a drunken stupor and seldom wholly sane. Whilst in this state, his morals sank lower and lower, and the time came when he became so degenerate that he was the very worst of the bunch. He was constantly seeking newer and more dreadful ways of exhorting the works of the Devil, even to the extent of sacrificing young babies and children at the break of dawn on a sacrificial alter by 'piercing them with a knife and tearing them asunder'. Whilst this was happening, the pagan onlookers danced around and chanted their weird laments until they reached a frenzy. Such were the depths of evil to which Simon had sunk.

Whilst these terrible deeds were being performed, a man who had been taking an awful chance by travelling alone in these parts during the hours of darkness, was attracted to the spot by the large fire and all the noise. He was horrified at what he was witnessing and seeking to save some of the children, he cried out for them to stop. A group of the men heard him and instantly seized him, but realising that he was on his own and could not present any danger to them, invited him to join in and have a drink and enjoy himself with them.

When he refused, they held him face downwards amongst the mangled flesh and carnage, which by now was almost knee deep, the stench was awful. They held him in this position until he suffocated, then carried on with their evil rites.

When the sacrifice of the children was finished and the men were well and truly drunk, they seized hold of one of the women who had been taking part, stripped the clothes from her, and marched her around the fire to the accompaniment of more frenzied chanting. When the singing and chanting had reached its crescendo, she was laid on the bloodstained alter, raped by a number of the men, after which they sent her to eternity by thrusting knives into her body.

Despite all the activities concerning witchcraft, that still continued despite the death of their main witch - the innkeeper's wife - the smuggling, well organised by the Frenchman - De Courcey, went on without a break.

One day, De Courcey arrived with his usual compliment of contraband, but he also brought a 'mummy' in a case, together with a quantity of embalming ointments, these being used a great deal on the continent. As this particular consignment was intended to be used for Black Mass purposes, the ointments were put into some porcelain vases which had also been stolen from the monastery.

The ointment would be used on the bodies of poor creatures who had recently been buried in the nearby cemetery whose graves had been unearthed and the corpses removed to the Inn. These corpses would be embalmed and stood around in a room, then misused by some of the evil ones according to their whim.

However, something which these exponents of malpractice were unaware was that amongst the ingredients of some of the embalming ointment, were also germs of the Plague.

Now although this terrible disease was quite prevalent on the continent, it was completely unknown on this island; but now the germs had arrived. As the ointment was used, so the germs were released and the disease spread like wildfire throughout the country causing a great loss of life, especially in London.

With the disease originating at the Inn, it was inevitable that some of the inhabitants should contract it, including Simon. He died, writhing in agony on the track only a few hundred yards from the Inn and those who were with him at the time, instantly recognising the cause of his contortions and fearing for themselves, fled back to the Inn, leaving Simon just where he had fallen.

As Simon lay dying, all his good and evil past flashed before him, and only then, did he realise just how he had been led astray by the old witch. By his own actions he had joined forces with the Devil to whom he had sold his soul, but now in these last moments he wanted to refute his bargain with Hell. Repenting there as he died, his last few words were in prayer "Forgive, forgive, oh Father, the deeds of evil you wrot I performed, and be pitiful unto this poor soul which cometh into Thy sight. As a little child, I cannot come, but even so, take me as I am and purge the evil from my soul, that I may repent unto all time in heavenly spaces wherein I am to be taken, but take, oh take, my Lord, I bitterly repent, repent of my evil ways and would undo the worst by coming to meet Thee on bended knee laid low upon my face, Father, I come, forgive." At that point, the last breath left his tortured body.

Later that day a stranger came along the track intending to spend the night at the Inn. When he saw Simon's body lying just where it had fallen and being a good Christian, he realised that he could not just leave the body there, so he said a prayer before looking around to find a small hollow to which to drag the body. He then managed to roll an old fallen tree trunk to the spot, with the corpse more or less covered. He again said a silent prayer and then carried on the short distance to the Inn, where he related his story to those who were gathered there.

Alas, by the next morning the goodly man was poorly rewarded for the previous days' good deed - he himself suffered and died of the deadly Plague which he had unknowingly contracted by touching the body of Simon.

After the people at the Inn recovered from the shock of these two deaths, some of them plucked up courage to go to the spot where Simon's body had been put to rest by the stranger, taking with them a slab of stone on which was scratched the following words. 'Here lies Simon, a monk of ill repute, but one who died in poor circumstances being laid low with the Plague itself'.

Can it be just coincidence that even today, some three hundred years after Simon's death, that a ghost of a monk can still be seen walking along the roads of what is now a built up area, heading in the direction of Treasure Holt.

KING CHARLES II AT THE INN.

However, back to our story and we now move on to another era. The evil innkeeper had died and the Inn, after being without a landlord for a couple of years and the evil doers having moved to a meeting place elsewhere, was now under the control of a good man and his family.

Times were still not good, but a change for the better could be noticed. Although at this period there was still a lot of unrest in the country, it was now Charles II who was being chased by Oliver Cromwell's Roundheads, and, once again, the Inn became involved.

Due to its isolated position, it was an ideal trysting place for the King and his band of Cavaliers and Charles often had meetings there with the Lady Staddon. Doubtless, many plots and intrigues were hatched at the same time.

One day a man on horseback arrived at the Inn and it was obvious from the dusty and lathered condition of his horse that he had ridden long and hard. He wanted a place where he could hide and lay low for a while. He had not been at the Inn very long when a Company of Cavaliers rode up, all dressed in their decorative costumes - they were searching for the man who was obviously a Cromwellian, and were determined to find him. The crafty innkeeper not knowing, or caring who would win the struggle for control of the country, and thinking of his own business, did not betray the man, but showed him a safe hiding place in the cellar beside the fireplace, the same cellar Matthew had used to hide his ill-fated box of golden guineas.

The Cavaliers searched high and low for their man, their voices and the crash of their swords against the wall echoed throughout the Inn, much to the consternation of the innkeeper in view of the fact they were causing a great deal of damage to the building with their spirited display of ardour to find the hidden man. He assured them that no such person was concealed on the premises, especially as the man they were seeking was one of Cromwell's men, whereas he was a staunch supporter of the King and all that he stood for.

"What say ye my gentlemen, lay your swords aside and drink with the house, as your Lord and Master has many a time. Greeting I give you, and wish you a safe journey hence on your weary and troubled way through the territory of these dastardly Cromwellians. Blast their bloody infamy, to Hell with them I say".

So the Company "partook and did eat and drink well", as they had also travelled many weary miles that day and they had a good rest as well.

When at long last they decided to leave, they realised that a lot of time had passed, and if indeed the fugitive had been there, by now he would be a long way away, and they would have little hope of catching him. Nevertheless, having eaten, drank and rested, and now feeling very good, so bidding the innkeeper farewell, they rode off.

Whilst all this had been going on, the hunted man had been just a few inches from where the Cavaliers had been seated having their meal, he had been standing there trembling with fear lest some sound might have betrayed his presence.

As can be seen, this innkeeper kept his peace with both sides, and for once an incident had passed at the Inn which ended without bloodshed.

However, the killings at the Inn had not ended. A Company of Cromwell's men later occupied the Inn and were laying in wait for King Charles 11 to join one of his many lady loves. On this occasion it was Lady Veronica and she had arrived at the Inn before Cromwell's men appeared on the scene. Obviously they had found out about the proposed meeting and thought that this time they could not fail to capture him. Although Lady Veronica could not leave the Inn herself to warn her lover, she managed to send a messenger to find and warn the King of the danger that awaited him if he came.

Sentries had been posted in the forest to cover all possible approaches, and it was one of them who, seeing a movement, shouted out the time honoured "Halt, who goes there", this was immediately followed by the crash of a musket being fired, and the sentry fell to the ground, dead. This was followed by a man dressed in fine clothes striding over to the prostrate form lying on the ground. He looked down and shook his head with regret at the killing he had just committed, but it had been a necessary one, there was so much at stake, indeed the King's life hung in the balance and at times, drastic action had to be taken in order to preserve it.

Pushing the body to one side with his foot, he worked his way through the shadows cast by the trees to where there was a sheltered bower set in a screen of roses, where he found the now very worried Lady Veronica waiting. Waiting for what, she did not know - who's footsteps did she hear approaching, was it her lover - the King, or was it one of Cromwell's men? It was with great relief that she saw it was one of the King's most trusted friends. Falling upon his knee and kissing her hand he besought her to go with him saying he would take her to where their Royal Master was anxiously waiting just a few miles away.

Taking his hand, she said they ought to leave immediately, as it was unsafe to linger for one minute longer than necessary. They threaded their way through the trees the way that he came, until they nearly reached the spot where the body of the unfortunate sentry lay, but to their horror, found that there was another sentry bending over the body. Not wishing to betray their presence and cause more bloodshed, they skirted around the area to where the escort had tethered his horse and mounting, galloped away at full speed to where the King was waiting.

THE END OF THE INN, THE END OF AN ERA.

Time moved slowly on and the Inn returned to its normal routine, until one day disaster struck. The Inn caught fire, and was almost completely destroyed, the innkeeper and his family perishing in the blaze. Had destiny at last caught up with the old Inn, considering all the evil that had been associated with the place. It was tragic that when a decent family had turned the tide away from the past, they should have suffered the fate which others had more than deserved.

Years rolled by and the remains of the old Inn and some of the forest were sold. Much of the remaining forest around was cleared and turned into farmland and the remains of the Inn were rebuilt as a farmhouse but, surprisingly, nobody stayed in the building for very long. One has often heard the expression "steeped in tradition" applied to some buildings and areas, but in this case perhaps "steeped in evil" would be more appropriate, as its past kept returning to haunt it; ghosts seen, screams heard, crops failed and eventually the place was abandoned as being hopeless.

Local residents have complained of a vile smell which appears and disappears as quickly as it comes. Could this be the manifestation from the carnage of the sacrifices or even from the decaying bodies down the well? Another strange thing which could be associated with Treasure Holt, a lane very close by, now known as Gorse Lane, which years ago was known as Gore Lane - Why? Could it have been so named because of the terrible rites of witchcraft carried out there or even the result of some of the bloody fighting that went on between the Roundheads and , this was the lane in which Simon the Monk met his end ! !

Once again, time passed and the old abandoned farmhouse was bought and turned into a private house, but, the ghosts that had been dormant for many years, had their slumbers disturbed, and they were not prepared to be pushed out of what had been their domain for hundreds of years ! ! !

UPDATE 1992

After all the trauma of the past years, Treasure Holt has now settled down to some semblance of a normal country house - well, almost - that is, apart from the odd female figure passing through the lounge to disappear through a doorway that has been sealed up for years, and of course the sound of footsteps going up the back stairs - but otherwise all is quite on the 'haunting' front.

Over recent years however, it has not always been so quiet and peaceful as the following stories will show.

Years of endless research and investigation have produced many weird and wonderful stories that can only help confirm some of the earlier stories.

Over the years there have been several reports of sightings of ghostly Cavaliers and Roundheads fighting on the lawn and the sur-rounding area, re-enacting their battle ! ! !

A late owner related that his mother often told of the time when she clearly saw the apparition of a Cavalier standing in their lounge and when she cried out in fright it just faded away before her eyes ! ! !

The same lady also recalled an occasion when a friend visited her one afternoon. Whilst she was making a pot of tea, the friend sat in the lounge just idly looking around at the old grandfather clocks - of which there were several in the room - and at the old spinning wheel standing in the corner, when she was shocked to see the figure of a little old man appear through the closed front door, clutching a box under his arm. He hurried across the floor to one side of the fireplace and gradually disappeared as if he were going down some stairs, then a few seconds later reappeared and going to the front door, opened it, only to be faced by a screaming mob who chased him across the lawn. Only then did she realise that despite what she had seen, there was no sound.

Could this once again be a re-enactment, this time though, of the murder of the unfortunate Matthew?

The late owner also had several of his own experiences to relate. Amongst them was the time when, lying in bed one Sunday morning, he heard a rustling sound going across his bedroom floor. Thinking it was his mother, he didn't take much notice, but when nothing was said he looked up and to his astonishment saw, not his mother, but the figure of a lady dressed in a beautiful crinoline dress or gown, slowly moving towards the open door and passing through it, just disappeared ! ! !

He also related when, on the evening of Boxing Day 1960, he was sitting in the lounge beside the fire with his mother and a friend of the family. As they were talking the figure of his father, who had died some four years earlier, appeared through the front wall where there was no doorway, walked half way across the room, stopped, turned around and stood looking at them for a full minute, then again turning, carried on slowly walking to the far end of the room where he appeared to pass right through the wall where years ago there had been a doorway.

The figure was dressed in the deceased's best Sunday suit, although when he died in hospital some twenty miles away, he had not worn that suit for a long time prior to his death. Another strange thing about the incident, was that although the owner saw everything, neither his mother or his friend saw anything ! ! He said that although it was Christmas time, they only had a few drinks and certainly not enough for him to imagine what he had definitely seen, also, he had certainly not been thinking about his father, so it could not have been his sub-conscious mind ! !

At various times there have been reports of strange occurrences at or near Treasure Holt, such as when one day some people talking outside, heard sounds of music coming from inside the house. Thinking this strange, they looked through the window and saw a lady with long blond hair seated near the fireplace playing a spinet, but when they opened the door there was nothing to be seen or heard ! ! !

There was also the time when a family, out for a walk one Sunday afternoon and passing the house, saw a lady with long blond hair, riding a white horse coming towards them. They moved to the other side of the road to allow them to pass, but on turning round to look again they found that both horse and rider had completely disappeared near the driveway of the house and although there was a clear view all round there was no sign of either, they had simply disappeared into thin air ! ! !

During its chequered history, there was a period when the Inn was frequented by highwaymen. It was an ideal place for them, secluded, plenty of woods in which to take cover and yet be able to watch out for the unwary traveller who would have to pass on his way to the Inn where most of them would be heading, or would just have left.

There was one particular highwayman who had been very successful in this area, but not content with just robbing strangers, he turned his talents to robbing the local folk who could ill afford to lose anything.

One day, after he had carried out a particularly nasty deed, the villagers decided that they had suffered enough at his hands. In the past they had at first appealed to him to leave them alone, but when this was ignored they threatened him, but again he took no notice. This was the last straw, they caught him and hung him from a tree on the corner of the lane leading to the Inn. Until recent years when the tree was taken down to make way for new houses, it was quite common to see the ghost of this highwayman still hanging from the tree, swinging in the wind.

More recently, some evidence has come to light which must add more weight to the 'Treasure Holt' story. In 1980 the then owner was carrying out some alterations to the house which included alterations to one of the chimneys. To his astonishment, concealed in one of the flues, he found two swords one of which was identified as definitely Cromwellian by a local antique dealer of high repute, the other was of similar period ! !

Further evidence that King Charles 11 had connections with the vicinity are bourne out by the fact that not far from Treasure Holt there is an old farmhouse, and examination of old Deeds reveal that this farmhouse and a quarter of the estate was inherited at one time by one of his mistresses - Barbara Villiers, and that after the Restoration in 1670, the King made her Duchess of Cleveland. Therefore there is every possibility that he did actually stay at the Inn.

It is recorded that Barbara Villiers died in 1709, aged 69.

An old local farm hand told the present owner that one of the oak trees in the grounds of Treasure Holt was so old that it was possible that Cromwell's men had sat under it's spreading branches and made up musket balls out of the lead stolen from the roofs of local churches.

At the time he took the matter lightly, but later he went over the area with a metal detector and to his surprise, only a few inches below the surface he found a quantity of lead cuttings and some tools that could well have been used to fashion the lead into balls ! !

One now wonders just what more there can possibly be to come to light in the future about the mysteries of Treasure Holt. Indeed, 'Treasure Holt' certainly is a real Treasure Chest ! !

Referring to the previous paragraph, since that was written, more facts have indeed come to light.

Regarding the token found by workmen under the floor in 1928 inscribed 'John Wilkins Iron Master 1793', further research reveals that in fact it should have read 'John Wilkinson Iron Master 1793'. Looking closely at the photograph of the token it is possible to see that a piece has broken off the edge taking with it the 'on' of Wilkinson.

Having identified John Wilkinson's 'halfpenny' token, the mystery deepens. What was his token doing in this area?

John Wilkinson from Shropshire, made his name and fortune from iron, in fact he was one of the major figures of the industrial revolution and invented a process for accurately boring out cannon barrels and later, steam-engine cylinders. He so devoted his life to iron and steel that he had his coffin and memorial chapel built of iron.

Being a wealthy man and employing a large number of workers, he, along with many others in similar position, found that when it came to paying their workforce it was impossible to obtain enough small 'regal' coinage for their wages. This situation was solved by producing their own copper tokens which were accepted by the local traders knowing their value would be honoured by John Wilkinson.

The mystery still remains "What was this token doing in this remote part of Essex, over 250 miles from where it was once part of an ironworker's wage?"

The Crinoline Lady

Matthew

Ghostly Cavalier and Roundhead fighting on the lawn

More Hauntings

THE MYSTERY OF THE HUMAN ARM

A Clacton man related a strange and most unusual story which he swears is true.

One evening in 1986 he took his dog for a run along the beach between Clacton and Jaywick and as so often happened, the dog ran off, only to make its own way home some hours later.

On this occasion however, it was nearly midnight before it scratched on the front door as usual to be let in. When the man opened the door, he was surprised to see the dog had something in its mouth; looking closer he was shocked to see it was a human arm that appeared to have been wrenched away from just above the elbow.

The fact that there was still flesh and skin on the arm suggested that it had not been detached for too long, also there were indications that it had been in the sea.

As it was now late, he decided to wrap it up and put it in his deep freezer overnight and to take it to the police station the following morning.

During the night the man and his wife were woken several times by strange rappings and loud moans and groans, which ceased as soon as he descended the stairs.

The next morning he took the arm to the police station, but this did not stop the moans, groans and rappings in his house. In fact they became more frequent and louder, almost as if when the dog brought the arm home it also brought home the ghost of its owner.

These noises continued for some weeks, then all went quiet for a couple of months. In the meantime the man decided to install a new central heating system, so his wife and his two children went to stay for a couple of weeks with relations on the Isle of Wight whilst he carried out the work for himself.

The first night the family were away, to quote the man, "all hell was let loose", rappings, banging, moans, groans all much louder than before. At first thinking burglars had broken in, he jumped out of bed, grabbed a length of timber and ran through the house shouting at the possible burglars to show themselves, but when nobody appeared, he then realised that the noises had stopped.

Similar incidents occurred over the next few days but gradually diminished in intensity until finally disappearing ! !

****

ST. OSYTH.

THE MYSTERY OF THE LADY IN WHITE.

A mysterious ghostly lady dressed in white has been known to appear at odd times in St. Osyth, but whether it is the same apparition reported by several bus drivers has not been ascertained.

One bus driver, making the last run of the day from St. Osyth to Clacton on a bright moonlight night was astonished to see the figure of a young lady dressed in what appeared to be a long white wedding dress waiting at a bus stop. He stopped the bus and opened the door for her to enter, but to his surprise there was nobody there.

The next day when he told the other drivers of his strange experience, some admitted that they had also seen the figure before but had said nothing about it as they feared that nobody would believe them or they would be ridiculed.

THE ROCKING CHAIR

A strange story has been related of an occurrence in the 1990's in a house in Clacton-on-Sea.

This large house was converted and let off as bed-sitting rooms. One of the rooms was occupied by a young man who it is believed, unfortunately, took his own life with an overdose of drugs. His lifeless body was found sitting in a rocking chair in his room.

This room was not re-let for some time, and the incident was never discussed and consequently forgotten. After some months the room was redecorated and subsequently occupied by a new tenant.

After the first night, the new tenant, recently arrived in Clacton after living for some years in the north of England, complained to the landlord that the room was exceptionally cold, which he felt to be rather strange in view of the fact that, coming from the north, he was used to the cold. There was also another complaint - he was being kept awake during the night by the movement and creaking of the rocking chair.

The landlord, respecting his tenant's complaints, duly supplied extra blankets and removed the offending rocking chair which he placed in another vacant room and peace reigned again.

A few days later, a new tenant took over the vacant room, but once again, the next morning, a complaint was made that the new tenant was kept awake by the incessant movement and noise of the chair.

Once again the rocking chair was replaced, this time it was exchanged for a chair in the landlord's teenaged daughter's room.

That night, within a couple of hours of the young lady going to bed, the whole household was woken by her screams. "That chair", she managed to blurt out. "It keeps moving and making awful noises".

The chair was immediately thrown into the back yard and the next morning it was stored in the garden shed, and that is where it remains to this day ! !

At least, in there, it can rock all night to its hearts content without disturbing anyone ! !

THE SOLDIERS STRANGE EXPERIENCE

In his younger days, Brian, a Clacton man was serving in the army in Cyprus. One day his unit was called upon to place sandbags around an unexploded bomb but, as he was putting a sandbag on the pile, the bomb exploded and the next thing he knew, he was in a military hospital bed in London.

After a few days, he began to be more aware of his surroundings and looking towards the bottom of his bed, was surprised to see the well framed figure of a paratrooper dressed in his No. 1 uniform standing there looking at him.

The paratrooper looked hard at him and said "You're in my bed". Brian, in his weakened state, fought to understand the situation and after what seemed ages, he replied that he was not aware that he was in the wrong bed, he had just woken up there, but he would have a word with the nurse or whoever came to attend to him next and perhaps they would move him to another bed.

The paratrooper turned and disappeared through the screens that surrounded the bed.

A short time later the ward Sister came on her rounds, seeing Brian awake she asked him how he was feeling etc. He then told her about the paratrooper. After a moments thought, she told him not to worry - she would take care of it.

Later that day Sister returned accompanied by the Matron. The Matron said "About this paratrooper, you must have imagined it, there was no paratrooper here. Now go back to sleep and forget about it". With that she left.

The next day, he received a visit from an Officer, a Medical Officer and a Padre all together. The Padre did most of the talking and he said "Regarding this soldier you saw yesterday, claiming that you were in his bed". "The description fits the last patient to occupy this bed, but he died four days before you arrived".

Apparently the paratrooper had been taking part in some night manoeuvres and had been badly crushed by a tank. He was not expected to live long and his parents who lived up north, were sent for.

Unfortunately, the man died a few hours before they arrived and his body was placed in the Chapel of Rest for them to see.

Could it be that he was aware that his parents were on their way to see him, and had tried to hang on to life until they arrived?

With this possible explanation, the Padre proceeded to carry out an exorcism service around the bed.

This was the first time that Brian had ever seen a ghost and he has often wondered if, as a result of his injuries, his psychic ability had been opened up, because, since that time he has been able to see many ghostly apparitions etc.

****

GT. HOLLAND

THE HEADLESS COFFIN BEARERS

A young man related a strange story his father had told him many times and he had no reason to believe it was other than the truth.

His father used to live in a cottage standing close to the level crossing in Pork Lane, Gt. Holland.

One summer evening his father stood looking out of an upstairs bedroom window just as the light was beginning to fade and to his amazement saw the figures of six men walking across a field in the direction of Clacton carrying a coffin, but what was even more startling - all six were headless ! !

HAUNTED THREE CHIMNEYS

"Three Chimneys", situated in the centre of Gt. Clacton village, dates back to the 1700's, possibly earlier, in fact it is one of the earliest farmhouses in Gt. Clacton.

It has now changed from a farmhouse to a guest house, but not all of its guests are "paying guests", some in fact are not even invited.

There have been several occasions when unexpected things have occurred that could not be accounted for; such as the time when it was snowing heavily and a snowy puddle and a couple of snow covered foot imprints appeared in the middle of the dining room floor. Now, this dining room is a fair size with a polished wooden floor and the casement door leading to the garden was locked and bolted as were all the windows. The only other possible entrance was through a door leading to the hall, yet there were just two snowy footprints and this puddle in the centre of the room. It just would not be possible for anyone to have entered the room without being seen, nor to have got into the position of the two footsteps without leaving other wet marks.

On several occasions visitors have remarked about the strong smell of violets, although there have been no flowers in the house nor had any scented air spray been used.

There was one occasion when, overnight, all the chairs in the dining room were taken from beneath the tables and placed upside down on top of the tables, not an easy feat, as it was difficult to balance the chairs in this position owing to their size and shape.

A large grandfather clock had to be chained to the wall to prevent a re-occurrence of the time when for no apparent reason it was flung to the floor, resulting in a very expensive repair.

At other times items have disappeared only to re-appear some time later in a different position. Although no one has claimed to have seen a ghost here, it is often felt there is a 'presence' and people have felt a 'something ' passing them on the stairs. There was one occasion when a visitor, a 'medium', remarked that she could feel a 'friendly presence' about the house and there was nothing to be afraid of.

One occupier was informed by a person who lived opposite the house, that one day whilst the owner was out, she could clearly see faces at the bedroom window overlooking the road.

In the cellar, there is a bricked up doorway which it is thought once led to a tunnel which, legend has it, connected with other tunnels leading to the churchyard, the Queens Head, the Ship, Eaglehurst and to Great Clacton Hall. But once again the question of tunnels is "another story".

JAYWICK
A LADY'S STRANGE EXPERIENCES.

A Jaywick resident related some of the strange phenomenon she had experienced in her house during twenty-one years she had spent there.

The house was built in the 1960's and as far as can be ascertained there was no previous record of anything untoward experienced by earlier occupiers, so it would be reasonable to deduce that the present occupiers have an above average psychic ability to see such manifestations or perhaps to attract various forms of phenomenon.

Although various things happened over a period of years, some are quite recent - there was an occasion in May 1992, when, at about 5.30 pm, she was standing in the stairway of her house and clearly saw a man's naked left arm suspended in mid air about four feet from the ground, it remained in the same position for about a minute before fading away.

Another time she came down the stairs and saw obscure shapes through the reeded glass panel in the lobby, these figures, possible three or four, appeared to be wearing Klu Klux Klan style pointed white hooded gowns. The figures appeared to be about five feet in height, moved across the room and disappeared. She recalled that the room temperature suddenly dropped noticeably. The time was about 9.30 in the evening

There was the time she saw white misty shapes not unlike giant ice cream cones moving across her lounge floor, her two cats followed their progress across the room with their eyes, but did not seem afraid of them.

On another occasion she clearly saw the apparition of a single wardrobe she recognised as one that used to belong to her father; it floated on its side about five feet off the floor of the lounge and then disappeared.

Many times when downstairs and alone in the house she has heard footsteps crossing the bedroom floor above.

One night her daughter who was 20 years of age, was asleep in her own bedroom when she woke up screaming that someone or something was pulling the clothes from her bed. She then went into her mothers room and went to sleep with her until the same thing happened again. There was nothing visible to account for either incident.

One evening at about 11.30 whilst looking out of her bedroom window she clearly a flying saucer in the back garden of a house three doors away. It was brightly illuminated and having its sliding door open, she could see three figures inside dressed in silvery like track suits and she estimated that they would be about five feet in height. She could also see what appeared to be a control console.

She tried to wake her husband so that he could see it, but by the time he reached the window it had gone.

When it took off, it went silently straight upwards after having been on the ground for about fifteen minutes.

When she looked across to the garden the next morning there appeared to be a circular indent in the area where she had seen the vehicle.

On yet another occasion, it was in February, about the time of the six o'clock evening news, the weather forecaster said that there would be a hard frost that night. Remembering that she had some washing still on the linen line, she went outside to bring it in.

As she went round the corner of her garage she saw a figure of a being, who she immediately thought of as an alien, standing with its hands upon a disused copper cylinder. It was of medium/small height, with blond shoulder length bobbed hair, a longish face with deeply recessed eyes, almost as if hollowed out of the skull.

She was not frightened by it, more overawed; it had longish thin arms with fingers that appeared to have tubes instead of nails. But the most unusual feature was its knee length boots, they were a clear material, not unlike a soft perspex and she could see the squareness of its toes which appeared to be as if two toes were webbed together, then a vee shaped space, then two more webbed toes.

The figure made a sweeping like gesture with its right arm, then crossed its arms across its chest to its shoulders, and then floated at an angle into the sky.

It is quite possible for the reader to dismiss this lady's experiences as a load of rubbish or stretched imagination, but in her defence, the writer would add that in his opinion she is a highly intelligent woman. Formerly an airline hostess, she speaks four languages fluently, obviously well travelled and has lived abroad in the Middle East on and off for over twenty-five years. One must form one's own opinion ! ! !

LT. CLACTON

THE GHOSTLY BIRTHDAY REMINDER

A lady from Harwich Road, Little Clacton, related how, when she was playing her organ one afternoon, she had a very strong feeling that she was being watched.

Knowing that she was alone in the house at the time, she disregarded the feeling and continued playing. However, the feeling became more intense, so much in fact, that she stopped playing and looked around the room.

To her utter amazement, sitting there in an armchair was the apparition of her next door neighbour who had died the previous October.

Prior to his death, it had been his habit to call round in the afternoons and sit in this very chair and listen to her playing.

By the time she had recovered from the shock, the figure had disappeared. This set her wondering as to why he should appear to her at this particular time.

It suddenly dawned on her that the next day would be the 30th June, his widow's birthday, and she hadn't thought to get her a birthday card. They had exchanged birthday cards for years and she would certainly have forgotten this one if it had not been for the timely return of the good neighbour ! !

****

TENDRING

THE MYSTERY LADY

A mysterious ghostly figure of a woman has been seen many times crossing the road that runs from the Cherry Tree Public House towards Weeley.

Customers leaving the inn at about ten-thirty at night after enjoying the 'spirits' within the house, find that they are then entertained by another type of spirit as they drive down the hill towards Weeley.

Although there have been reports of sightings at this spot for many years, the figure still appears, and there were reports of it being seen three times within a month in July 1992.

The origin or reason for this manifestation unknown.

THE HAUNTED BUNGALOW ON PLOUGH CORNER

A bungalow at Plough Corner, Little Clacton, is said to have been built over the point where two 'Ley Lines' cross. The bungalow was built about 1961, possibly on the site of a much earlier building.

The point where Ley Lines cross is thought to be an area of great magnetic energy and this force is believed to have various 'magical' powers. Sick animals have been known to seek out such spots and lie down on them, later to stand up apparently fully recovered.

It is also thought that these crossing points are areas of great pyschic energy which often enable manifestations to take place. This could account for the pair of phantom hands that have been seen floating across one of the rooms in the bungalow.

Perhaps it is the magnetic energy from these Ley Lincs that causes the temperature to suddenly drop, cause the lights to flicker, make the television picture tremble then fade away, and cause the electric switches to switch themselves on and off, or could it just be some playful spirit testing out the energy it has just picked up ! !

Legend has it that a gibbet once stood on the site of the building, and a man was hanged from it in the 17th century. This could possibly account for the ghost of a highwayman or robber, seen appearing about the house, either as a complete misty figure or just a pair of hands. The full figure was last seen about 1985/86.

Sometimes voices can be heard throughout the building, doors open and close of their own volition and often three knocks occur before the kitchen door opens of its own accord. Sometimes the television will switch itself on and off.

There is a 'regular' ghost who visits the occupants; they call it Derek and they always know when he is about or has been. Knives go missing from the drawer, sometimes they fly through the air to stick into the kitchen door, other times they turn up in odd places, sometimes days later.

The occupiers believe they know who 'Derek' was. They think that he was a friend, who took his own life on Holland marshes some years ago by stabbing himself in the heart. He always appears at 6.30 pm 26th. February, the anniversary of his death ! !

MYSTERIOUS U.F.O. ACTIVITY IN THORPE ROAD, GT.CLACTON.

Although reported sightings of Unidentified Flying Objects seems to be a long way from the realms of Ghosts and Hauntings, but when considered, both subjects have a lot in common - both have their disbelievers, neither have been accepted by science, neither can be reproduced or made to appear on command etc. etc.

No doubt with the passage of time the mortals of this planet will fully understand both matters and wonder just how ignorant we could have been in this day and age.

In the meantime we can only ponder on reports on both subjects from eye witnesses , and there certainly seems to be no shortage in either case.

Both phenomena tend to occur at odd times and often seem to return to their respective areas of visitation, but not always in quite the same form or circumstances, which makes it difficult to predict their appearances.

A classic example of this is the sighting of a possible U.F.O. in the vicinity of the Thorpe Road, Gorse Lane and Tan Lane areas of Great and Little Clacton.

The first report dates from September 1962. A Clacton man was travelling on his motorcycle at about 11.30 pm along Thorpe Road, Gt. Clacton, when the tools in his pannier started to rattle. Pulling over and stopping beneath a street light opposite where Gorse Lane meets Thorpe Road, he secured the tools and was just about to carry on with his journey when he was suddenly aware of a huge shape rising from behind the small clump of trees and scrub then on the corner of Gorse Lane prior to the building of private homes.

There was no sound of any kind, although the 'thing' was so large that the man described it as "large as a football pitch". It was incredible.

Without any more ado, he jumped on his 'bike and rode off at top speed towards Thorpe. As he travelled along the road the shape appeared to be following him directly above his head, but so low that he felt if he stood up on his motorcycle he could touch it!

Arriving at the top of Thorpe Road he turned into Tan Lane and switched off his lights and carried on in the moonlight, hoping that he would lose the 'thing'. However, he soon came to a sharp 'S' bend and was forced to slow down and put his lights back on. To his horror, the 'shape' was still hovering above him .

Reaching Harwich Road where he lived with his father, he rode straight through the front gate without stopping and into his garage

Running to the house, he was 'greeted' by his father wanting to know what all the noise was about at this time of night. Pointing to the sky they were both able to see this huge shape heading towards Thorpe-le-Soken station at high speed, to disappear in the distance ! !

****

Some ten years later, two men were returning by car from London at about 9.30 pm. Travelling along Holland Road, from the direction of Little Clacton and just before they reached the junction withThorpe Road, they both saw a pair of lights across the fields. Thinking they were coming from a tractor working late, they paid little attention until they realised that the lights were rapidly coming closer and were not in the field, but up in the air ! !

As they turned into Thorpe Road heading for Clacton, the lights were now so close and the 'object' had turned parallel to them and had slowed down to about their speed.

Looking up through the car's nearside window at an angle of about 45 degrees, they could clearly see two banks of lights, similar to those of a double-decker bus, but much larger.

Continuing along Thorpe Road the 'shape' followed them, until they turned left into Gorse Lane and stopped in a layby about a hundred yards into the lane.

Both getting out of the car, they were astonished to find the 'thing' was now stationary directly above them, it was so huge and low it absolutely blotted out the sky and neither of them could see the edges which would have enabled them to determine its actual size.

They could see two or three slightly diffused coloured lights on the under side, also there was a whirring noise coming from it, similar to the noise made by a 10 h.p. electric motor.

All this was too much for them, they made for their car and sped off home ! !

****

About 1985, there was a further report of a sighting of a U.F.O. in this same area, details are not to hand at the time of going to print, but by all accounts the general story is much the same.

In 1992, the farmer who owns the lane opposite Gorse Lane, narrated that although he did not actually see a U.F.O., he was awakened one night a couple of years back, by the sound of his horses becoming restless in the stables. Fearing that somebody was tampering with them, he hurriedly got out of bed , dressed, and went across the yard to the stables, but could find no reason for them to be disturbed; everything appeared to be in order. Spending a few minutes talking to them to calm them down, he locked the door again and was about to cross the yard, when he became aware of a whirring noise, like a large electric motor, coming from behind the barn.

Retracing his steps he crept along the side of the barn, but was only half way along when the noise stopped. He continued to the corner and peered cautiously round it, but although it was bright moonlight he saw nothing to account for the sound ! !

This farm is situated within a two hundred yard radius of previous sightings, therefore one cannot ignore the possibility that this sound was from yet another U.F.O.

****

THE MYSTERIOUS MIST OF THORPE

A man, his wife and young daughter, having just moved from London to Thorpe-le-Soken, were having their first look around the Church.

Having entered from the Weeley end, they proceeded to walk past the church tower into the churchyard. They were just about to turn behind the church, when they were astonished to see a mist emerging from the wall of the building adjoining the churchyard. It appeared as a giant ice cream cone of swirling steam, and passed along behind the church about shoulder height, still keeping its swirling motion. Having passed the end of the church, it turned sharply to the right, following the path towards the old part of the churchyard where it disappeared.

Shortly after this incident, the family went inside the church where they saw the vicar. They told him what they had just witnessed, but he played it down, almost suggesting that they had all imagined it ! ! !

One wonders if there could possibly be a connection with the 'ball of mist' two young girls saw bounding along the road near the War Memorial over 50 years ago ??

Maybe somebody else has seen this apparition as well ? ?

APPARITION AT MEADOW WAY, JAYWICK

The wife of a Colchester shopkeeper related the occasion when in 1969 she, a young bride, and her husband had just moved into a rented furnished bungalow in Meadow Way, Jaywick.

Being their first home, they were both very excited and considered themselves extremely lucky to have found such a place so quickly.

The first day they took possession, they brought their few treasured possessions and moved in.

They spent most of the evening arranging the furniture to their requirements and generally getting settled in . The time came when they thought of going to bed and while her husband went outside to check he had locked his van, she went into the bedroom and started to undress. It was then she glanced at the full length mirror on the open wardrobe door and to her horror she saw the reflection of an elderly woman standing in the doorway. Letting out a scream she turned round, the figure was still there as solid as in real life. Completely shocked and stuck for words, she just stood there opening and closing her mouth, words would not come.

Her husband came in through the back door and locked up and it was not until he called out to his wife that the figure slowly faded away. Who she was and why she returned that day nobody has ever found out, but the couple soon found another house and moved out ! !

****

THE PELDON ROSE

THE LANDLADY'S EXPERIENCE

The fearless ex-landlady of the Peldon Rose public house related the time when, as she was walking along the road towards Mersea in daylight, she found herself accompanied by the figure of a Roman soldier who remained at her side for almost two miles before he disappeared.

Although she said that she was not scared, she was never-the-less apprehensive, but having heard many stories of other people having seen and heard phantom Romans in this area without coming to any harm, why should anything happen to her!

DEDHAM

THE BIRCHWOOD HOTEL MYSTERY

Several members of staff claimed to have seen a shadowy figure in one of the bedrooms where a murder was said to have been committed, but the mystery that caused more trouble than the manifestation of the ghost, was the blood on the carpet ! !

Every time the carpet was cleaned and shampooed, the bloody patch returned and eventually it was decided to replace it, but after a few days the stain reappeared.

In the end the management decided to have a section of the floor taken up and replaced with new floorboards, and for the new carpet to be turned around so that the stain would be under the bed.

For some months everything was back to normal - until one day a chambermaid spotted a reddish stain appearing. Thinking that one of the guests had spilt something she tried to wash it away, but the more she washed, the worse it became.

Faced yet again with this problem, the management decided to close off the room completely, hoping no doubt that in time a remedy would be found.

In fact "time" did provide the answer - the company went into liquidation and the new owners demolished the building for redevelopment ! !

****

ST. OSYTH.

GHOSTLY LEGS

One evening a lady was driving her mother home from Point Clear to St. Osyth. As they approached the sharp bend in the road where the road branches off to Wigboro Wick, they were both astonished to see a ghostly pair of mans legs striding along the road.

They were so close to the corner that neither had the opportunity to take a real long look at the legs, but both agreed it was definitely just a pair of legs - no body ! ! !

ARDLEIGH

STRANGE GOINGS ON AT THE CROSS INN

Over the years the old Cross Inn at Burnt Heath, an old hamlet between Ardleigh and Great Bromley, has seen many changes and landlords.

At one time the landlord was a 20 plus stone heavy weight boxer - Frank Goddard. In his heyday he ranked with the best of British boxers and even fought for the championship. His idea of training would be frowned upon by todays boxing trainers; he certainly did some road work - with a pick and shovel, and at times he did a little running - from pub to pub - to replace the fluids that he lost in his running.

But this big man, for all his toughness, was seldom seen without his two Pekinese dogs whom he adored, and of course, the contrast emphasised his size.

But long since Frank's days at The Cross Inn, it has become a Motel and has also collected a mischievous ghost who delights in playing with other spirits in the beer cellar.

The present owner has many a time been baffled when his beer pumps failed to work, and on going into the cellar found that several of the taps had been turned off, not just finger tight as a normal person would turn off the tap , but so tightly turned that it has often been necessary to use a large spanner to turn them back on - could it possibly be the ghost of Frank Goddard returning to do the job he must have done so many times before ??

The strange thing about the beer cellar is - there is only one key to the door, and the owner always has it on his own key ring. Many times when going into the cellar he has been aware of someone or something watching him, and at times when turning around quickly was sure he caught a glimpse of a large shadowy shape standing in the corner ! !

****

CLACTON

THE GHOST OF A SOLDIER

There is said to be a ghost of a soldier who appears on the site of the old Butlins camp near to the Martello Tower. It is thought that he may have been killed in a fight in the now demolished ballroom.

ROWHEDGE
YE OLDE ALBION PUBLIC HOUSE

One of the oldest public houses in the area - Ye Olde Albion, at Rowhedge, has a strange story associated with it - one that includes smuggling, murder and haunting.

Around about 1750 a ruthless gang of young smugglers used the small enclosed Snug Bar of the Albion as a meeting place to plan their operations. The local Customs and Excise officer was in their pay thus ensuring that there would be no interference from that direction also they were kept informed, well in advance, when other officers would be in the district.

Late one evening there was a violent quarrel between the gang and the Customs officer; he was demanding more than his fair share of the proceeds.

In his temper the unwise officer threatened to hand them over to his superiors in Colchester - a very dangerous thing to suggest in his circumstances. Smuggling was a hanging offence.

In a fit of rage at the mere suggestion, the merciless gang seized the officer and determined to silence him there and then. They soon produced a couple of strong ropes from one of their boats and tied up the unfortunate man with one whilst a noose was prepared in the other.

As soon as the noose was ready, they put it around his neck and the other end of the rope was passed through a ring in an oak beam in the Snug ceiling. It was only a matter of minutes before he paid dearly for his outburst.

Many times since that fateful day, the ghost of his swinging body has been seen dangling from that same ring in the bar.

Locals say his ghost still roams around the Albion, dressed in the red uniform then worn by the Customs Service, especially in the area where the corridor used to be that passed the Snug Bar.

Ghostly footsteps are often heard pacing the upstairs floor when the pub has closed for the night and all is still, also at times a child's cry has been heard in the area of the toilets, but so far, for this, there is no explanation.

****

THE GHOST WITH A DUSTER

A few years ago a father and his two sons, all very keen cyclists, were out for a Sunday afternoon ride. They travelled from Colchester to Lexden then along Chitts Hill as far as West Bergholt.

Reaching the White Hart public house, they headed towards Nayland; about half a mile along the road they passed a lady walking in the same direction as they were travelling. From the rear she appeared to be middle-aged, wearing a navy blue skirt, with a whitish blouse and as she was not wearing a hat they could see her short fair hair. In her hand she she was holding a yellow duster.

About a quarter of a mile further on, to their utter astonishment there she was again, the same woman, still with the yellow duster in her hand steadily walking along. There was just no way she could have overtaken them, there was no turning off or short cut that she could have taken. A few hundred yards up the road they stopped and discussed the matter, but the lady did not catch up with them and they did not see her again.

They came to the conclusion that what they had all seen could only have been a ghost, perhaps a victim of a car accident, but why the yellow duster ? ?

THE HAUNTED NURSES HOME

It is a well known fact that whenever there is a group of young women in the age group of 12 to 22 years of age in fairly close contact with each other i.e. a girls boarding school, or in this case a nurses home, collectively they give off some form of psychic energy that attracts or feeds all sorts of phenomenon.

The Nurses Home in Lexden Road, Colchester, is no exception to the rule. For many years there have been whispers of strange 'goings on' there; many a young student nurse has run screaming with fright from her room in the middle of the night, only to be told that she has just had a bad dream or a nightmare, both of which often occur in the early days of a nurses training and is generally accepted as one of the hazards of the job until such times as dealing with illness, surgery and sometimes death, becomes part of their lives.

That explanation is quite plausible and usually accepted, but at other times the poor girl just knows that there was something else.

There is one room in particular that is kept locked and is only used as a last resort when all the other rooms are occupied. In fact, for a while it was only used as a 'guests room' for people staying for only one night. Often that one night was more than enough for them.

This bedroom has a door with a reputation of locking the occupant in, then suddenly unlocking itself and swinging open of it's own volition.

On one occasion, a visiting nurse was given this room for the night and knowing nothing of it's reputation she retired about 10.30 pm. She had not been asleep long before she was rudely awakened by having the sheets pulled from her, but thinking that she must have turned over and drawn the sheets with her, she remade the bed and went off to sleep again.

It was not long afterwards that she was again woken by the sheets being ripped from her and then to her amazement, she was tipped out of bed by some unseen force, and the bed remained on it's side.

Switching on the light, she just caught a fleeting glimpse of a shadowy figure with a sickly grin on it's face standing by the upturned bed.

This just was too much for her, she hastily dressed and spent the remainder of the night in the nurses lounge with all the lights switched on!!

THE HAUNTED NEW POLICE STATION

Many times people have raised their eyebrows when told of a relatively new building having a ghost. Unfortunately, the general belief is that only old houses are haunted, but this is not so, only the odds are greater because their age increased the chances of something having occurred within the building with a resultant haunting.

However, a classic example of a new building acquiring a reputation of having a ghost within a year of it's existence is Colchester's new Police Station, just off Southway.

Built in the late 1980's on a site previously occupied mainly by terraced houses and an old engineering works, the Police station was designed to include an underground car park, but during the excavations some unrecorded tombs were discovered.

Shortly after this discovery 'strange happenings' began to occur - footsteps were heard walking along the passages, shadowy figures began to appear in some of the rooms and papers and files began to disappear, only to re-appear later. (Mind you, this used to happen a lot in the old Police Station as well ! !)

One of the most affected areas is in and around the boiler room. In fact, as soon as one enters this room there is an overpowering feeling of oppression and shadowy figures have been seen dodging between the racks of files stored there.

In the corridor leading to the cells and a section where stray dogs are temporarily housed, there is an area where the temperature suddenly drops and dogs literally have to be carried past this spot..

Many times unexplained footsteps have been heard approaching the Traffic Wardens Office, then stopping outside the door, but when the door is opened there is nobody there ! Strangely, the footsteps are always heard approaching the door, but never going away.

****

THE WILSON MARRIAGE SCHOOL MYSTERY

An ex-student of Wilson Marriage School, Barrack Street, Colchester, related that when she attended the school, several fellow students as well as herself witnessed a trapdoor leading to the bell tower rising a falling for no apparent reason, when it closed it did not fall with a bang, but seemed to be slowly lowered as if by some unseen hand.

THE GHOSTLY HORSEMAN IN THE SKY

A strange story was related by a family from East Mersea concerning their strange experience one afternoon in 1980.

They were on their way by car from East Mersea to visit a relative in a Colchester Hospital. Being 'locals' they knew the easiest and shortest routes through the lanes to avoid the holdups in Mersea Road due to major road works then taking place.

Turning off the Mersea Road, having just passed over Manwood Bridge, they followed the winding lane which used to pass by Berechurch Hall Road near Military Corrective Training Centre. (The old army 'glasshouse').

About half way along this lane they were surprised to see a grey shape looming up some fifty yards ahead of them. As they got nearer, the shape turned out to be a leaping horse with a rider who could well have been a First World War soldier He appeared to be looking straight ahead, obviously a tall man, sitting very upright in the saddle with his legs straight down in the stirrups.

He was wearing a greyish uniform with a sash which could well have been a Sam Brown belt across his chest, and on his back was a large pack.

His hat was an Australian style with a turn up on the left hand side, this turn up was held in position by a badge of some sort.

In his right hand he held an upright staff which extended a couple of feet above his head and attached to the top of it was a triangular pennant being blown backwards by the wind.

He was holding the reins with his left hand and hanging from his left side was a long sword.

The strangest thing of all was, this apparition appeared to be some forty feet in the air, jumping over the trees and just under the very low cloud; the horse seemed to be at full gallop just clearing the trees in three leaps.

THE SEQUEL

A retired Colchester man kept a secret both to himself and his family for many years, fearing that if he confided in anyone they would not believe his story and would ridicule him. But eventually the time came when he decided to divulge his secret, come what may, but in doing so he was unaware that he would be confirming a story related some years earlier.

Working at the Military Corrective Training Centre as a boilerman, it was his job to ensure that the boilers supplying the camp with hot water were well stocked and serviced.

Owing to the nature of his work he was required to start at 4 am. One morning he was cycling to work and had just ridden through Roman Way Camp and turned left into Berechurch Hall Road, when suddenly a horse with rider jumped over the hedge just in front of him, galloped across the road and disappeared over the hedge on the opposite side of the road.

He got off his bike, somewhat shaken and it was only then he realised that there had been no sound of hooves on the road, in fact, there had been no sound whatsoever ! !

Remounting his cycle, he reckoned he broke the world sprint record to reach his place of work ! !

The Military Corrective Training Centre is brilliantly floodlit during the hours of darkness, and as he was heading towards it, he was able to get a good sight of both horse and rider in the short time available.

The rider appeared to be wearing a bluish uniform with what seemed to be a three cornered hat and a cape flowing from his back.

The whole episode took a matter of only a few seconds and at 4 o'clock in the morning, seeing something like this is not the best time to notice too much detail, but when one considers the similarity to the previous story - the area, the horse and rider, the uniform, the hat, the direction - could they be one and the same?

THE MYSTERY OF THE BATHROOM DOOR

In the early 1930's a row of semi-detached houses were built in Old Heath Road, Colchester. One of these, was later occupied by a man and his wife together with their eleven year old son.

They had been living in the house for only a short time when one Saturday night, soon after they had all gone to bed, heavy footsteps having a strange hollowness about them, were heard coming up the stairs, followed by the sound of the bathroom door being opened with such a force that it crashed back against the wall.

The father called out and asked if the boy was alright, and not to make so much noise; the lad replied that it was not him making the noise, he was in bed.

His father got out of bed and went through the house, finding nothing out of place he returned up the stairs shutting the bathroom door as he passed, and back to bed.

A couple of hours later exactly the same thing happened - footsteps up the stairs followed by the crash of the bathroom door. The father once again jumped out of bed, ran on to the landing, just in time to see the bathroom door swinging to and fro, but there was nobody there to have caused it ! !

The rest of the night passed without further incident, in fact the next couple of weeks were trouble free, then the following Saturday night there was a repeat performance - footsteps and bathroom door banging.

The following day the father saw his next door neighbour in the garden and asked if he was aware of anything unusual having happened in the house since it was built. The neighbour replied that some time previously a man had committed suicide in the bathroom by tying a rope around the door knob and hanging himself.

Needless to say the family soon moved out. This story was recounted in 1933 by the man who was that eleven year old boy.

****

HALLOWE'EN NIGHT LEGEND

About a century ago it was an Essex belief that if one stood by the church door at midnight on Hallowe'ens night it was possible to see the shadowy figures of those doomed to die in the parish during the next year.

THE MYSTERY OF THE LANDAU

In the early 1970's a workman travelling to work from Mersea Island towards Colchester turned into Berechurch Hall Road. About two hundred yards ahead he was astonished to see six horses drawing what appeared to be a golden Landau carriage; and even more unnerving was the fact there was no sound of hooves or wheels.

The whole thing was only visible for less than half a minute, but the memory was so etched on the man's mind that he used to shake whenever he had to travel along that section of the road.

****

THE DISAPPEARING MAN

A sergeant from the Military Corrective Training Centre in Berechurch Hall Road, Colchester, related an incident which occurred when he was going off duty early one morning to his civilian billet.

He left the M.C.T.C. by a foot path which passed through the small wood behind Berechurch Hall heading towards Bounstead Road. In the distance he could clearly see the figure of a man walking in the same direction but at a much slower pace.

Thinking it rather unusual for someone else to be using this path at that time of the morning, he soon caught up with the man and slowing down to the same pace started to pass the time of day with him. After a couple of minutes he realised that he was holding a one-sided conversation and looking round was startled to find that the man had vanished into thin air and he was by himself !

STRANGE OCCURRENCE AT A BERGHOLT ROAD SHOP

The wife of a shopkeeper in Bergholt Road, Colchester, recalled a strange occurrence there a few years ago.

Her husband was out one evening at a meeting and she was alone in the upstairs flat. Half way through the evening, she definitely heard footsteps walking across their bedroom floor.

It was only a small flat and to get to the bedrooms anyone would have to pass through the living room. As she had not left the room all evening it left only two possibilities, it was either burglars or a ghost.

Not taking any chances, she picked up a heavy torch and edged her way into the bedroom, but there was definitely nobody there and looking into the smaller bedroom, again - nothing.

A little later, the same noise was again heard crossing the bedroom floor. All was quiet for a few minutes, then a chilling wind swept through the living room, down the stairs and into the shop, followed by a crashing noise in the rear of the shop.

Once again picking up the torch, she bravely went into the shop, where fortunately the lights had been left on and she was able to see the back door which opened outwards had been forced open, despite the fact that it was locked and barred.

Going into the yard she could see nothing to account for the noise or damage to the door. The yard was completely enclosed by a high concrete block wall and a pair of doors over six feet in height.

Back in the shop she looked around, but could see no sign of any thing missing and nothing out of place, even papers on the counter were still undisturbed despite the strength of the wind down the stairs ! !

It would appear that the wind wound it's way down the stairs, through the shop and made it's exit through the back of the shop.

Nothing she was aware of had previously happened in the shop or flat and the only connection she could think of was the death of her mother three days earlier ! !

****

ST. OSYTH

There is said to be a friendly ghost that appears in a cottage in Mill Lane, St. Osyth. It opens doors during the day, but when it pays a visit during the night it always leaves a crust of bread on the kitchen table.

EARLS COLNE

THE HAUNTING OF THE COACHMAN INN

Earls Colne's Coachman Inn has a relatively young ghost, 'young' as opposed to an ancient haunting, although there may well be a few of those as well about the inn.

The present landlord had only been at the inn for a few months when his son and daughter-in-law together with their two and a half year-old son came to stay for a few weeks.

Many times during the day when the child was supposed to have been asleep in the bedroom, the parents heard him laughing and talking to himself. Thinking that this was something all children did, they were not unduly concerned.

One day his grandmother went upstairs and hearing the child talking, quietly opened the bedroom door. The boy was sitting up in his cot looking towards a corner of the room and still chattering away. When he spotted his grandmother he stopped speaking and when she asked who he had been talking to, the boy pointed to the corner and said "that man, who is he?"

She did not tell him she could see nobody there, but very carefully asked if he had seen the man before. The boy told her that he always came to see him and sometimes played with him.

When the young family went home, the grandparents moved into that room whilst their own room was being decorated.

Forgetting about the young boys story, they slept peacefully in the room until one morning the grandmother, on getting out of bed, went over to the window to draw the curtains. As she turned around, she was shocked to see the figure of a young man in his early twenties, dressed in a singlet, jeans and trainers. He stood in the corner of the room just looking at her; a smile came over his handsome young face and then he gradually faded away.

Waking her husband, she told him the story of their grandson and what she had just seen. At first he told her she had imagined it, but later thought that there might just be something to the story - and left it at that.

Several months later, a young couple called and over drinks the young man mentioned that his father used to own the inn and that he had been brought up there.

The landlord, remembering his wife's tale, cautiously asked him if he knew anything about the place being haunted. The youth visibly paled and replied that it was because of the haunting his father had moved out.

Recovering his composure, he then asked what they had seen, and where. The landlord related the whole story as far as he knew it; the youth confirmed the sighting of the young man in the bedroom and went on to explain that the figure that had materialised was in fact his brother who had been killed in a motorcycle accident outside the inn, and that bedroom had been his room.

Naturally the family were devastated at the loss of their eldest son, but shortly after the accident his apparition started to appear in his old room and down the stairway.

All this was too much for the family so they had sold the inn and moved away, hoping that time would let them forget their tragic loss.

****

AN OLD STORY FROM COLNE PRIORY

There is a story dating from Crowellian times concerning Colne Priory, in fact it was almost a legend even in those days.

A part of the old Benedictine Priory where the servants had their quarters was said to be 'troubled' by the clanging of the Great Bell at two o'clock every morning , thus preventing the servants from having a good nights' sleep.

At one time during the Civil War, Cromwell's Roundheads occupied the Priory and it was not long before tales of the bell reached the ears of Cromwell's Officer in Charge.

Being a man of strong Puritanical beliefs, he chastised his men for believing such rubbish and to prove his point he ordered his equipment and bed to be placed in the servants quarters for him to sleep there that night.

Retiring just before midnight he soon slipped into a deep sleep. Dead on two o'clock in the morning he was awakened by the sound of the bell, scrambling out of bed he lost no time in running back to his old quarters, and the matter was never mentioned again in his presence!

STRANGE HAPPENINGS AT A HARWICH RESTAURANT

A restaurant in the centre of Harwich, could almost qualify for the title of the 'most haunted house in Harwich'.

Although covering a relatively small area, the name - Harwich - is known the world over, due mainly to fact that at onc time it was the most important naval port in the country, ships from all over the world having berthed there.

With such an historic record and the fact that at one time there were more than 22 public houses, plus ale-houses, it is not surprising that many a tragedy occurred, some of which have left imprints not only in the atmosphere but on buildings as well.

Whether or not any historical tragedy happened within the walls of the restaurant it is not recorded, but it is known that a man did hang himself in the cellar many years ago, and that the house on one side had to be exorcised a few years ago, and even more recently a ghostly figure has been seen crossing the road to disappear into the house on the other side!

But our story really concerns the happenings in the restaurant between 1990 and 1992. Previous owners experienced some psychic activity - unexplained footsteps on the stairs and the sighting of a lady in one of the bedrooms.

The sighting was during the night when the wife got out of bed to see if her two children were sleeping all right in the next bedroom; on her return she was just about to get back into bed when she became aware of a female shape standing near the window. Although the figure did not move, for some reason she found herself ducking to avoid it. When she looked up the ghost had disappeared, but at no time did she feel frightened despite her automatic reaction. The present owner's wife has also twice had a similar experience.

The present owners relate the occasion when they were woken up about 2 am by the sound of footsteps coming up the stairs. Thinking that their two sons (both in their late 'teens) had been to a local 'night spot' and were coming home later than they were allowed, the owner got out of bed and went down the stairs to the first floor lounge. seeing the door open, he looked inside but finding nobody there, closed the door behind him and next looked into the bathroom. Again there was nobody there, so closing the door he next looked into his office opposite the bathroom, yet again there was no sign of the boys.

Going down the stairs to the ground floor, he checked the back dining room and the kitchen with the same result - nobody. He next went into the front cafe/bar and finally down to the cellar bar - all with the same result - no one.

Going back up the first flight of stairs he suddenly heard the lounge door opening. Now, the lounge had recently had a new carpet fitted and a draught excluder fitted to the bottom of the door scraped the carpet when the door was opened, so there was no mistaking the sound.

He thought, -"I've got them"! ! The lounge door was open, but when he switched the light on there was nobody in the room ! !

Climbing up the second flight of stairs he looked in both the boys bedrooms, there they were, sound asleep ! !

One morning when he and a friend were in conversation in the rear dining room and their attention was suddenly drawn to some bottles standing on the floor - a partly used bottle of Martini in particular. Suddenly the remaining contents started to 'percolate' and thinking that there had been a vibration from the wooden floor, they stamped on it but it made no difference. When they checked the floor underneath the bottle they found it was standing on an old concrete hearth ! !

Another time he was talking to a customer in the front bar, when he felt something tugging at his shirt collar. Thinking that his wife had crept into the bar from the back door and was having a game with him, he turned quickly round with the intention of grabbing her - but there was nobody there ! !

One evening there were ten customers in the cellar bar when a picture on the rear wall started to move backwards and forwards of its own volition, not a swinging movement side to side, but a forward and backward motion.

On another occasion a young lady's coat had been hung on a hat and coat hook in the cellar bar, when all of a sudden, witnessed by several people, the coat was literally thrown across the room ! !

It was in this cellar that the man was said to have hanged himself, maybe his spirit does not approve of its present day use ! !

Upstairs in the dining room a large mirror was thrown from its position on the wall - it didn't just fall down, it was thrown some six feet into the room ! !

One day the owner's mother-in-law was washing up in the downstairs kitchen when she felt a definite nudge on her back, she looked up expecting to see someone standing behind her, but there was nobody there. Continuing with the washing up she next felt a distinct push in her back, enough was enough, she hastily made for the back door and went outside.

Then there was the time when the owner was hoovering the hall and was bending forward when he was aware of someone or something pushing past him and disappearing into the rear dining room. Thinking that it was one of his sons, he called out, but there was no reply and later it turned out that his son was actually in the kitchen some fifty feet away and hadn't been anywhere near the hall ! !

Another previous owner told of also hearing footsteps on the stairs and also several times hearing heavy rappings on the windows both upstairs and down. These rappings came from outside the building and were so loud on one occasion that he opened an upstairs window and shouted for whatever it was to go away ! !

****

THE HAUNTED HOLLY TREES MUSEUM

One evening, a caretaker was working late in the Holly Trees Museum, Colchester, when he distinctly heard heavy footsteps crossing the floor above him.

Knowing he was supposed to be the only person in the building and that he had locked the door behind him when he came on duty, his first thoughts were that somebody had either been locked in or had broken in.

Being a fearless man, or to put it as described "he was a man who drinks pints", without hesitation he strode up the stairs ready to challenge whoever should be there, but to his amazement there was not a soul in sight.

Not satisfied with his first search, he went through the whole building again, but with the same result - nothing that could account for the footsteps.

The only conclusion that he could come to was that the place must be haunted.

We hope that you have enjoyed reading 'THE TERRIBLE TREASURE HOLT STORY' also the 30 Ghost stories.

But have you also read its companion books -

'HAUNTED CLACTON'

and

'THE HAUNTED COLCHESTER AREA'

Both books now available at most book shops and newsagents or direct from

Wesley's Publications, 61 Lymington Avenue, Clacton-on-Sea,

CO15 4QE. Price £3. 95 Post free.

Shortly to be published

'THE GHOSTS OF BORLEY'

PLUS

30 STORIES OF GHOSTS & HAUNTING ON THE

ESSEX AND SUFFOLK BORDER.

The publishers would welcome any stories or experiences of Ghosts and Hauntings in Essex or Suffolk for future books.